REVISED EDITION

The New TA for KIDS

for

(and grown-ups too)

Powerful techniques for developing self-esteem

by Alvyn and Margaret Freed

Art Director — Rick Hackney
Text Illustrations — Rick Hackney
Cover Art — Sue Treckeme

JALMAR PRESS, PO box 370, Fawnskin, CA 92333   To Order:(800)429-1192 T:(909)866-2912
F(909)866-2961 info@jalmarpress.com   online catalog: www.personhoodpress.com

D1257741

Other Materials by Alvyn M. Freed, Ph.D.

TA for Tots (and other prinzes)
TA for Tots, Volume II
TA for Tots Coloring Book
TA for Teens
KID PAC
TOT PAC

The New *TA for KIDS* (and grown-ups, too) is a totally revised and re-illustrated edition of the original *TA for KIDS* (and grown-ups, too).

14th Printing, 1983 — 5,000
13th Printing, 1982 — 10,000
12th Printing, 1980 — 12,000
11th Printing, 1979 — 15,000
10th Printing, 1978 — 25,000
9th Printing, 1977 — 25,000 — 3rd edition
    (revised)
8th Printing, 1977 — 3,700
7th Printing, 1976 — 25,000
6th Printing, 1975 — 25,000
5th Printing, 1974 — 25,000
4th Printing, 1973 — 20,000
3rd Printing, 1972 — 10,000 — 2nd edition
2nd Printing, 1971 — 2,000
1st Printing, 1971 — 1,000

ISBN: 0-915190-09-5
Library of Congress No. 77-81761

Acknowledgement is made to the International Transactional Analysis Association for permission to reprint John James' "The Game Plan" from Vol. 4, No. 3, 1973, Copyright 1973 by ITAA.

Printing No.: 26   25   24   23   22   21   20   19   18   17

TABLE OF CONTENTS

iv

ACKNOWLEDGEMENTS

A lot of water has flowed since *TA for Kids (and grown-ups too)* was written and published in 1971. Our hope in this revision is to incorporate some of the new and exciting ideas produced by the many OK people who have been writing about TA since then. Our first acknowledgement and regret is that Dr. Eric Berne could not have lived to share the delight that old and young people have expressed when encountering, perhaps for the first time, his ideas here in *TA for Kids*.

Second, we wish to acknowledge all the creative people in the International Transactional Analysis Association (ITAA), the organization created by Eric's genius and warmth. His inspiration has led so many of us to open up and use our intuition and creativity.

Third, we wish to express appreciation to John Dickinson Adams, Editor-in-chief of Jalmar Press, and Bernadine Hoff, friend and critic, at whose urgings we are revising the original book.

Appreciation goes to Betts Hackney for her patient and expert typing of the many drafts and to Rick Hackney for his wise editorial suggestions and encouragements while simultaneously doing his professionally excellent job of illustrating the book so effectively.

Finally, to all of you who express your confidence in and love for us and thus make our task a labor of love, we say thank you.

Al and Marge Freed

P.S. As you undoubtedly have noticed, the "I" of the first book has changed to "we" in the current revision. I have invited Marge to join me in authoring the book, just as I have invited her to do many things with me these last thirty years. I am truly honored and delighted to have her as my coauthor, colleague, and wife.

Alvyn M. Freed

FOREWORD
((For People in Charge)*

When I wrote *TA for Kids (and Grownups Too)* in 1970-71, literature describing Transactional Analysis consisted of Dr. Eric Berne's original books and Dr. Thomas Harris' *I'm OK, You're OK* and the ITAA bulletin articles. *Born to Win* (James & Jongeward) was yet to be born. Since then, TA, the exciting method of understanding oneself and others in order to improve one's interpersonal relationships, has inspired an ever-increasing number of books and articles.

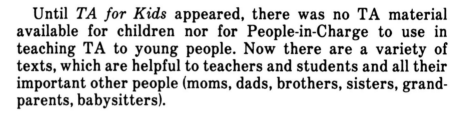

Until *TA for Kids* appeared, there was no TA material available for children nor for People-in-Charge to use in teaching TA to young people. Now there are a variety of texts, which are helpful to teachers and students and all their important other people (moms, dads, brothers, sisters, grandparents, babysitters).

I feel, however, that *TA for Kids* still fills a need unmet by other materials by speaking directly and simply to people aged 9-13 (approximately grades 3 through 7) in words they can understand. I am reaching out to young people of all ages, who need to be tough enough to ward off the "discounts" of an outrageous world and flexible enough to enjoy a fulfilling childhood. I believe such a fulfillment is essential in the process of experiencing a healthy, satisfying total life experience.

Many of you People-in-Charge have indicated that *Kids* has served to clarify for you the basic concepts of TA and to make them useful in your daily lives. This is thrilling to me and I thank you. Such expressions validate my effort to bring TA to everybody. Since 1970, TA as a viable, ever widening wave of knowledge has spread throughout the world. Creative people have expanded (and expounded) its concepts. In this revised version of *TA for Kids (and Grownups too)*, I have again attempted to "keep it simple" and to "say it so an eight year old person can understand it."**

I believe the revision will provide youngsters with the basics of the TA knowledge they need to help to understand themselves, to cope with their own feelings and the feelings of other people in their world.

Many people have been kind enough to write and express their reactions to *TA for Kids*. Happily, many have expressed their delight and I am grateful and well stroked by this.

---

*(or for Grownups, in the title of this book)

*This term is used to replace parents or adults or grownups. Each of these terms tends to make younger people feel as if they are sub-human beings.

**Eric Berne

Many suggestions for revisions have been received and I have considered each one carefully (and, I hope, objectively). For example, the use of the terms MEP, MEA and MEC, meaning Me the Parent, Me the Adult, and Me the Child, while originally intended for emphasis, has been criticized as being confusing and awkward. These terms have been eliminated in this revision.

The image of the Parent has been enhanced and clarified in line with current thinking, to emphasize the OK nurturing Parent and the OK critical, controlling, and protective Parent.

The book can serve as a manual for teachers as well as a text. Each chapter fits nicely into the usual classroom period, including the exercises and "tests" at the end of the chapter. There is usually time for informal discussion in the last ten minutes of the period, with social interactions related to the chapter.

The "tests" are usually used as the basis for discussion so that success is guaranteed and failure minimized. The teacher can use this as a means of evaluating the learning which is taking place.

I sincerely hope that the revision will continue to delight and educate the audience for which the book was originally intended.

I also hope that the book will be more useful to PIC's who have the responsibility and joy of participating in the development of children.

INTRODUCTION TO REVISED EDITION
(For the Kids, in the title of this book)

This book is to help you feel OK. Because you are OK and always have been. By understanding yourself better, by understanding and accepting your own feelings and the feelings of other important people in your life, you will get back the good feelings about yourself you may have lost and begin to trust yourself again. When you learn this, you'll probably get along better with other people and be happier, because you'll like and trust them.

Does that sound like something you'd be interested in? I hope so — because you can be happier, do better at home and school if you take care of your feelings and those of other people. Remember, when you were born, you were OK and you still are.

There are many ways to learn about yourself but the one I think is easiest and best is called Transactional Analysis (that's the TA in the title of this book). Do you know what a transaction is? Here's one example: When you go to the store, you give the salesclerk some money and he or she gives you the notebook you are buying. That is a business transaction. You give something and you get something. It's an exchange.

So a verbal transaction between people is the same — you give something, (words, for example) and you get something back, such as words, a smile, a nod, or maybe a frown. Whatever makes us aware of another person is called a stroke, and an exchange of strokes is called a transaction. For example, you may say, "Hi, Beverly." Your friend Beverly says, "Hi, Marian" to you. Or maybe you put out your hands and your friend "slaps" your hands in greeting.

Well, that's what a transaction is — an exchange of strokes between people. But that's only half of Transactional Analysis.

Analysis? That means figuring out how something works, how it is put together, or how something is done. For example: if you figure out how to do an arithmetic problem, you have "analyzed" the problem. If you analyze a transaction, you figure out what is going on at the time in terms of feelings, yours and the other person's. So Transactional Analysis is figuring out transactional exchanges between people.

I first wrote this book because all through my life I have wished I knew how to make and keep friends. I've also wanted to have others like me and to avoid getting people I love angry with me. Lots of people have told me what to do about it but no one ever taught me how. TA has helped me and I feel it can help you, who are much younger, to do it sooner and better. I hope so.

CHAPTER ONE
Who Are You?

You are three people. You thought you were just one. No, you're really three. Oh, not a person with three heads, nor are there three little people running around inside you. But, inside each of us, you and me, we have three different parts and they act like three different people. These three people make you and me do what we do. They're as different as you and I are different. For you and me to understand ourselves, to know why we do what we do at different times, we have to get acquainted with our three selves. We have to know these three people pretty well.

THE THREE PEOPLE INSIDE OF US (P - A - C)

The three people inside of you and me are called Parent, Adult, and Child. You didn't know you had a Parent inside you, but you do, and I do, too. There is also a part of you and me which we call the Adult. This is the wise self in us which thinks and knows how to make decisions. And then there is a part of us we call the Child. Both young and old have a Child in them. This is where we all live and feel. The Child occupies a great deal of our time and makes many "right-now" fun decisions. Like — let's go swimming.

I was surprised, and I'll bet you will be also, to learn that your mother and dad, and all older people like me, also have these same three people inside them. By getting to know the three "inside" people — Parent, Adult, and Child — we'll get to understand and love the other important people in our lives.

The Parent in you believes and behaves very much like your mother and father believe and behave. But *all* the people who are important to you when you are very young help to form the Parent in you and the way they were affects the way you are now. Can you name a few who helped form your Parent? Mother, father, grandmother, grandfather, baby sitters, teachers, big brother, sister — anyone else?

The Parent in me is sometimes *very bossy* but at others I'm a *very kind and caring* person. I like to help people. What is your Parent like (not your mom or pop) — the big "P" Parent inside you? Write down some of the Parent ideas (Parent tapes) and save them for later.

The Parent in each of us tells us what to do, how and when to do it. Sometimes it's pretty bossy; at other times, Parent is helpful and kind. "Come here this instant," or "Go to your room," are things mothers and fathers sometimes say. Then we learn and say them later to other people like brothers and sisters just as if we were mom and dad.

The Parent also takes care of us and likes to do things for others. When the phone rings, my Parent will say to my wife: "Sit still, I'll get it." That's my Parent taking care of her.

Or her Parent will say to our son when he comes home from school, "How about some iced tea and a peanut butter sandwich, hon?"

Does the Parent in you like to do things for other people? Help them and protect them? Talk about that. What do you like to do? Why?

Does your Parent sometimes tell other people what to do or what not to do? Let's talk about that, too.

While you are reading this book and answering some of the questions at the end of the chapters, the Adult in you is in charge. The Adult is the part of you which thinks, learns, and figures things out.

Your Adult makes sense, decides what to do, and keeps the other two parts of you out of trouble by looking ahead and avoiding trouble, if possible. Can you think of some ways your Adult works? Write them down, right now.

By the way, have you noticed that when I write about the Parent or Adult, I use a capital "P" or "A"? That's because in TA those words have a special meaning. Parent in TA language doesn't mean mothers and fathers and Adult doesn't mean grownups. These are parts of your personality. When we mean mother or father as your parents, we use a small "p."

The third part in each of us is the Child — and that is a very strong part of you and me. The Child in me acts very much like I did when I was very young. Looking at me on the back cover you'd never believe I was three or four once, but I was. I had young feelings and young ways of acting because I *was* young and little, and I felt strange. Somebody said I acted like a little man from Mars, discovering Earth. I felt like that, too.

I used to like to play with my dog and talk to him. Do you? He'd chase me and I'd run around on all fours, just like him. Mother would say, "Oh, now you're being a puppy dog." Even now I sometimes growl and bark at a dog if he is barking at me and that's my Child having fun again.

We have a cat named F.F. He and I play by making cat sounds. Do you do that? Fun, isn't it? That's the Kid in me (Child) playing.

What are some other things your Child likes to do for fun? How about your mom and dad? Do they have fun with you? If so, you are lucky because your Child and the Child in them can have fun together. If not, maybe their Child needs some love. After a while we'll talk about how to *stroke* the Child in others and help them feel good.

There are all sorts of feelings inside my Child: happy feelings, sad feelings, angry feelings, hurt feelings, excitement, make-believe people, and so on. Do you ever feel sad, hurt, angry, or afraid? Talk about that right now. The feelings we have are all part of the Child in each of us.

No matter how old we are — 6 or 60 — we will always have these three people inside us. That is why it's helpful to find out more about them in the next few chapters.

EXERCISES

1. Who are you? Discuss.

2. Name the three people or parts inside of us.

3. In TA terms, what is the difference between a Parent and a parent? (I know it's the capital P, but what does it mean?)

4. From what you've learned so far, why is it important to you to know about the three people inside of you?

5. What is the P in you like? The A? The C? How do you behave when one or the other is in charge?

WORDS AND IDEAS FOR YOUR ADULT

Parent
Adult
Child
Parent tapes

CHAPTER TWO
About Strokes: Warm Fuzzies and Cold Pricklies

In the introduction to this book, we talked about transactions. You may recall that a transaction is an exchange of strokes. A stroke looks like this.

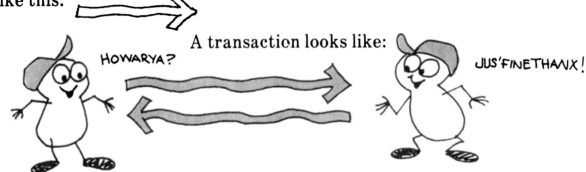

A transaction looks like:

HOWARYA?

JUS'FINETHANX!

Now we are going to learn that there are several different kinds of strokes — some we like and some we dislike.

WHAT IS A STROKE?

A stroke is any sort of act by someone else that lets you know they are there: a smile, pat on the back, a whistle, voice, anything like that. Have you ever noticed how dogs and cats like to be petted, fed, played with, and talked to? You and I are the same way. When we were little we were touched, held, bathed, tickled, swung, talked to, and played with by mom and dad. We liked all of this because it felt good. These are things that people do to us that cause us to feel. They are called "strokes" in TA language.

Tell the person nearest you about some of the strokes you get that make you feel good — a hand on your shoulder, a hug, a handshake, a smile from a friend. Dr. Claude Steiner, in a new book called "A Warm Fuzzy Tale" names pleasant strokes "Warm Fuzzies"* because you feel warm and fuzzy all over when you get one. He calls unpleasant strokes "Cold Pricklies". Dr. Steiner first wrote about Warm Fuzzies and Cold Pricklies a long time ago. Now he has a little book about them which I think you will enjoy. It has lovely pictures by JoAnn Dick.**

THIS IS A WARM FUZZY

SOME WELL KNOWN FUZZIES

HELLO FUZZY   COMPLIMENTARY FUZZY   SMILE FUZZY

The Warm Fuzzies we have listed so far are mostly touch strokes. There are other kinds of Warm Fuzzies, too — a "hello," a compliment, a warm and friendly look, a smile. What we say and the way we look at each other as well as the way we touch each other can all be pleasant strokes (Warm Fuzzies).

*From Steiner, Claude — The Original Warm Fuzzy Tale, published by JALMAR Press, Sacramento.
**Dick, JoAnn, illustrated TA for Tots, by A.M. Freed, 1973

FREEBIES ARE THE BEST KIND

The very best strokes are the ones you don't have to earn — the strokes you get from people important to you just for *being*. These are free strokes. These strokes are not only for being good or for being clean or for being smart or for winning — (these are Warm Fuzzies, too, of course) but just for being you — a boy or a girl — a Prinz (Freedian for Prince or Princess). For being Marianne, George, Amy, Jesse, Mark, Marge, Larry, or Al (all the members of our family).

When someone says "I love you," or "I like you" or "You're a neat guy," you feel good and that feeling is a Warm Fuzzy. A hug makes you feel the same way if you let it.

Some of us think the only way to get Warm Fuzzies is to earn them — by getting good grades, winning, or doing things for people. There's nothing wrong with getting these kinds of strokes because we all need strokes in order to stay alive. But the best kind of Warm Fuzzies are just for being.

Another way to get strokes is to ask for them. And they're OK too. They're just as good as earned strokes. "Please tell me you like me." Or "Tell me again how you liked the back rub I gave you." Strokes are vital to your physical and mental health and you need them every day to be healthy and happy.

MARASMUS — THE SPINE SHRIVELER

Babies will die if they don't get warm and loving strokes. One time doctors and nurses in a big hospital discovered that some babies died because they were not being lifted or cuddled or cooed over. They seemed to give up wanting to live, and some stopped living. They died of an illness called marasmus.*

At the same time, the doctors discovered that the babies who were cuddled and stroked grew strong and healthy. From that time on the doctor told the nurses to stroke the babies. All the babies were stroked and nobody got sick.** Older folks need strokes just as much and most of us spend our lives seeking them.

Do you like strokes? I do. What's your favorite Warm Fuzzy? How do you like to be stroked — a back rub, a smile, an "A" on your report card, or what? Talk about it now. Talk about that with your mother today.

MY FAVORITE WARM FUZZY IS_____

*Deterioration or shrivelling of the spinal cord due to lack of stroking.
**Ref: Berne, Eric, M.D., *Games People Play*, Grove Press 1964
***"Tender Loving Care, 4 times daily". This now appears on charts for new-born infants in all hospitals.

COLD PRICKLIES

Sometimes we get other kinds of strokes which make us feel bad, but which keep us alive if we're not getting Warm Fuzzies. Maybe we get slapped or whacked on the bottom or yelled at. These are strokes too. They are negative or unpleasant strokes. They make us feel, but they're not Warm Fuzzies. Dr. Steiner* calls these strokes Cold Pricklies. Sometimes when we think we can't get Warm Fuzzies, we'll work to get Cold Pricklies. Any stroke is better than no stroke.

Have you ever been given Cold Pricklies? What happened? Talk about it.

*Ibid Steiner

When I was a little boy, sometimes I thought my little brother was getting too many Warm Fuzzies and I wasn't getting enough. So I would do things like spill my milk or whine at mother. She might get mad at me but at least she knew I was there and had to give me some kind of stroke. These were earned Cold Pricklies, negative strokes. Have you ever done anything like that? Talk about that with somebody.

Here's a secret I am going to share with you. Everyone wants strokes so the more strokes you give other people, the more you will get. Sound like a good deal to you?

EXERCISES FOR GROUP

In this chapter you have learned about strokes, good strokes, hurt strokes, earned strokes, and free strokes. How do you get your strokes? Talk about this. What kind do you get most? From whom? Who do you like getting strokes from? How come? What do you do to get them? Is this the best way?

1. What is a stroke?
2. Why do we need strokes?
3. What kind of strokes are there?
4. What is a free stroke?
5. Tell how to earn strokes.
6. Give somebody a Warm Fuzzy.
7. Are all strokes pleasant?
8. What is a Cold Prickly? Why do you sometimes seek them when they feel bad?
9. What will probably happen to you if you give lots of strokes?
10. What is a Prinz?

EXERCISES IN STROKING

Here are some exercises to try out on your little sister, brother, or even mother or daddy.

1. Tell someone something nice about himself and watch him smile. You'll be stroking his Child.
2. Another exercise in stroking (doing a nice thing) is to be sure to call five people by their names today — people that you don't really know — and watch what happens when you say their name.
3. If you want to find out how it feels to get strokes, get four or five people to call you by your name.
4. If you really want to have fun, touch (lightly) some people that you like and get them to touch you.

These exercises are for your Adult with fun for your Child. You'll find that you'll enjoy them.

WORDS AND IDEAS FOR YOUR ADULT

1. Transactions
2. Warm Fuzzies
3. Cold Pricklies
4. Earned and free strokes
5. Positive or pleasant strokes
6. Negative or unpleasant strokes
7. Marasmus
8. Prinz

CHAPTER THREE
The Parent — Critical and Nurturing Me

In the first chapter we talked about three people inside of us. We called them the Parent, the Adult, and the Child. Now, today we are going to talk more about the Parent. When we were little, we needed mother and daddy to teach us what to do.

> ATTA BOY,... NOW DO THE OTHER LOOP... RIGHT!

We also learned a great many things from them that they didn't know they were teaching us.

Like getting angry, or hitting others, or taking care of others, or giving and taking, smoking or drinking while they teach health, love between parents, hugging others. They taught us how to be mothers and fathers, men and women, husbands and wives by doing the things they did. When we heard them talk or yell at each other, we learned that that's what husbands and wives do. In this way, we learned how to speak to each other, how to be kind or cruel, calm or excited, friendly, loving or cold.

WHERE DO WE GET PARENT TAPES?

When you were very little, you may have played with dolls. Maybe you still do. As part of your play you spanked the doll. Who did you learn that from? Or you played house and you wanted to use dad's or mother's clothes and dress up and act like a big lady or gentleman.

Now that I've gotten older, I sometimes act the way my father acted. That's my Parent. When you see and hear yourself acting like your mother or father would act or would want you to act, that's your Parent speaking.

WE NEED A PARENT

The Parent is a good part of us. We could not get along without our Parent. Your Parent tells you what to do when your Child is puzzled.

Sometimes you've heard daddy say things like, "Children should be seen and not heard," or when he gives you a spanking he says, "This hurts me more than it does you." Which part of daddy is talking? Right. His Parent! Why? Because that's what his father said to him and he learned about being a Parent from his father. When you hear yourself saying to someone else, "Don't talk back to me," or "You're bad," or "That's stupid," or "You're ridiculous," or "Do it because I say so" it's the Parent speaking. When you find yourself using those kinds of words, it's really mother or daddy speaking through your mouth.

Parents may also say things like "You're the most beautiful child in the world" or "What a good boy or girl" or "You are so helpful" or "What a lovely smile." And we remember these words too.

We call these kinds of sentences "Parent Tapes" because we hear them just like tapes on the tape recorder. What are some of your Parent Tapes? Proverbs and old sayings we use as guides are Parent Tapes. These have been handed down from one generation to the next. Most of them we learn from our mothers and fathers, grandparents, teachers, and other important people.

19

CRITICAL AND NURTURING PARENT

The Parent has two parts: One part criticizes us, controls us, protects us, punishes us, and bosses us. This is the Critical Parent (CP). The other part which is helpful, loving and caring, feeds us, helps us, gives us things, approves, supports and encourages us, does things for us. This is the Nurturing (nur-chur-ing) Parent (NP).

Both are important to us.

The bossy Critical Parent (CP) acts like and says many of the same things our real life parents say or do. The CP is the one who lets us know when we are doing something wrong like hitting someone else, stealing something, being late, talking back, swearing, and stuff like that. Often the CP tells us how and when to do "right" things: to say "Please," "Thank you," to share with others, to use a fork and knife in the "right" way. Most parents want you to be an honest, considerate, well-behaved person and think that criticism and direction will help you. Most mothers and fathers try to teach us by telling us what to do, what not to do, or how to do it. They also may threaten or spank us to help us "do what's right." They aren't usually being mean; they just hope they can help you learn to do things "right."

The loving and caring part of the Parent is called the Nurturing Parent (NP). The NP is the one who takes care of you in a loving way, gives you what you need or want, allows you to have fun, reassures you when you are afraid. NP tells you you are OK just because you are.

What are some of the things your mother does like this? How about dad? When do you use your Nurturing Parent? These are some ideas to talk about in class or in group or at home with your important people.

Maybe now that you are older you can begin to use your Nurturing Parent on yourself. You are OK and you must begin to take care of your feelings. Love yourself and take care of your own needs.

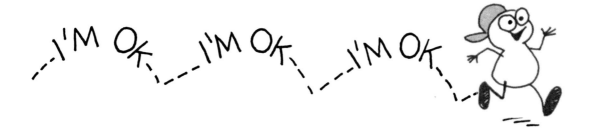

You'll find if you begin to like and trust yourself that liking and trusting others becomes easy. Soon others like and trust you and that's what this TA business is all about. Talk about how you can take care of yourself.

Here are some ways:

Ask for what you want.

Don't say "no" if you mean "yes" (Say "yes" if you want a second helping of spaghetti — instead of letting your CP say "don't be a pig").

Tell yourself: "You're OK even though you failed the test," or "Even though you struck out and missed the big chance to save the game, you're still OK."

Give yourself permission to express your feelings in a straight way instead of "swallowing" them.

Try saying: "I don't like it when you _____." or "I get angry when _____." Avoid saying: "You make me so mad!"

Own your own feelings.

Allow yourself to have and express feelings of fear, sadness, joy, fun, anger, pain without feeling guilty.

EXERCISES FOR GROUP

Complete the sentence or underline or circle the answer you think fits best. See Page 100 for the ones I think fit best.

1. P stands for the _____.
2. P tells (a) P, A, or C what to do when (b) P, A, or C is puzzled.
3. When daddy says, "Don't talk back to me," his _____ is speaking.
4. The _____ Parent is sometimes bossy or critical.
5. Write down some of your Parent Tapes, like: always _____ Never _____.

6. Tell whether CP or NP is talking:
   a. You're being silly. _____
   b. You're lazy. _____
   c. Don't do that. _____
   d. Stop that noise. _____
   e. Go to bed this minute. _____
   f. Children should be seen and not heard. _____
   g. Poor child, she's so shy. _____
   h. She's such an adorable youngster. _____
   i. Here, darling, eat this nice cookie. _____
   j. Daddy knows best. _____
   k. Honesty is the best policy. _____
   l. You tell me the truth and if there's any lying to be done, I'll do it. _____
   m. Be careful when you cross the street. _____
   n. I'm afraid you'll get hurt. _____
   o. I'll take care of you. _____
   p. You're a good guy. _____
   q. Would you like a nice glass of milk? _____
   r. I'll help you do the dishes. _____

WORDS AND IDEAS FOR YOUR ADULT

Parent Tapes
Critical Parent
Nurturing Parent
Coming on Straight

I think, therefore I am.
— Descartes

CHAPTER FOUR
The Adult — The Thinking Me

The three people in us are the Parent, Adult, and Child. Dr. Eric Berne called these three people — states of the self, or Ego states. Ego means self.

Well, if the Parent Ego part of us is a tape recording of mother and dad, how do you or I begin to think for ourselves? How do we do math, for instance? Here are three circles to represent the three people in us:

Right in the middle of our three circles is one labeled A for the Adult Ego state. And that's a good place for it to be because the Adult is the thinker, the one who figures things out and decides things. The Adult (A) gets the facts, learns them, and makes sense when we talk. The Adult collects and stores facts and figures out answers to problems. Hopefully, in school, A learns enough to get us A's (grades, that is). Of course B's are OK, and C's aren't all that bad either.

THE ANSWER IS "NONE OF THE ABOVE"

ADULT IS LIKE A COMPUTER

The Adult works like a cash register or an electric computer. For instance in the grocery store, the clerk pushes the buttons on the cash register for each thing you buy. Then he/she pushes another button, wheels whir and then zoom — out comes the total for all those things you bought.

Other computers add, subtract multiply, divide or handle facts, words, or ideas. Your Adult is like a computer — in go the facts, round they go, and out pops the answer, but faster than any machine. That is, if you use it a lot. The more you use your Adult, the better it functions. Just like a muscle that gets stronger when you use it.

Your brain is a bigger and better computer than any of the machines that are built by people. I recently read that a big company had built a computer to handle one million bits of information. Your Adult (your brain) can handle a billion bits if it has to. Your Adult can build a computer but no computer can build a "you." How about that?

CONTAMINATION OR GETTING "MESSED UP"

You *can* learn anything you want to, anything your Adult decides to learn. You are using your A when you read this book. But if your P or C "messes up" your computer, you won't learn anything. When an Ego state, like the Adult, is "messed up" by another one, like the Child, we say it is contaminated.

For instance, if you are hungry and thinking about a hamburger while you are reading, your A doesn't have much of a chance against your strong hungry Child feelings. (See next chapter.) If your P is saying "That's just a bunch of junk," your P is messing up your A's chance to learn.

Maybe somebody you believe in told you: "You're just like me, you have no head for figures." So your Child leaps on that when it's math time.

PUT YOUR A IN CHARGE

How do you keep your C comfortable while studying? Here are some ways. Short periods of concentrated study, with frequent rest or fun breaks. Use snacks and restroom breaks. Make sure the light, air, and temperature are right. Keep noise level down. No music. No "fun" people around during studying time. This is all taken care of by your Adult.

Your A can decide what to do, like when to listen to your P tapes or when to let your C have its way. Each of us, no matter how old, has a good-sized efficient A in us. Otherwise we couldn't have learned to walk, talk, or dress ourselves, to read and write and do arithmetic, to throw and catch a ball, to decide and plan what we're going to do. Some people do one thing well, others do something else. There's no need to be perfect. Some people practice using their Adult. Others let other people do their thinking for them. Which are you? Why?

Here are some words and actions which will help you know the "A" in you:

Read this book

Answer the questions

Decide what to wear today

Work on a Scouting merit badge or some other project

Choose to save your money or spend it

Decide to take a study break

Decide to study and then do it

Know when you've learned the task and check it

Plan an outing, party, or visit

Read for fun

Read to learn

Decide to clean your room

Decide you can solve the problem and do it

Choose to play a while

WORDS AND IDEAS FOR YOUR ADULT

Adult

Computer

Eric Berne

Ego State

Contaminated

Messed Up

Though I'm a child and I am small, my feelings are not small at all.
— Harriet Bird
from "Songs of the Warm Fuzzy"

CHAPTER FIVE
The Child — The Feeling Me

When we first used the word "child" in this book, we meant a little boy or girl. Now we are using it to mean the part of us which "feels." And we will use the capital letter "C" — Child — to show the difference.

I FEEL A SONG COMING ON!

Do you hear a noise? Feel a breeze? Did you ever smell buttered popcorn? (Good, huh?) If you say "yes," it was your Child in action. Do you ever get scared? Laugh? Like to swim? Get angry? Feel mad, glad, sad, or bad? These are all things that your Child does.

THE CHILD IS ALL-POWERFUL

The Child is one of our most powerful parts. The Child feels but is not too strong on thinking or planning so it needs some control and protection. Our Adult and Parent take pretty good care of the Child most of the time. But sometimes the Child willfully does what it wants; like eating sour apples and getting sick, or staying up too late and getting too tired to get up on time, or getting hurt by doing thoughtless things. This gives all three parts of us a problem. The Child gets sick, feels bad, or is in trouble. The Parent may be disgusted or worried and the Adult may be puzzled or in despair over what to do.

When we talked about the Parent in each of us (Chapter Three) we learned about the Critical Parent and the Nurturing Parent — two parts of the Parent, both important to us. The Child has three parts like this:

A ADAPTED
LP Little Professor
FC FREECHILD

and again, each one is important to us.

THE NATURAL OR FREE CHILD

Let's start with the Natural Child. This part of the Child is free; free to laugh, cry, giggle, sulk, be happy or afraid, to love and hate, to be impulsive, to play and have fun. The Natural Child sometimes is called the Free Child. A baby cries or laughs, sleeps, plays with its toes whenever it wants to: that's the original Natural Child in each of us. And if you or I have fun and let out our other feelings when we feel them, that is our Natural Child too, no matter how old we are.

Sometimes we say words or make sounds like a little baby or an animal, just for fun. Let's make some now: cat, dog, pig, cow, baby. Fun,

isn't it? That's your Child.

Your Natural Child *feels* and wants good feelings, food, milk, whatever, right now! Very demanding. Also gets scared or hurt, cries and screams.

THE LITTLE PROFESSOR (LP)

The LP is the thinking part of your child and often acts to get what the Child wants. It's clever and original. LP makes up things, like stories, games, or unseen playmates. It loves to draw pictures, act, and play make-believe. LP invents things out of daydreams. You may make believe that you are an airplane, a beautiful or handsome magazine model, a great athlete, or an astronaut. People-in-Charge (PICs) sometimes call this daydreaming. If it weren't for daydreaming, there'd never be any inventions. So it's OK to daydream sometimes — and to act out the dreams.

Of course it takes study and work to make some dreams come true. Thomas Edison, the greatest inventor of our age, once said that invention is 1% inspiration (dream) and 99% perspiration (work). What do you think he meant?

Your Little Professor knows how to get grown-ups to give you what you want. A baby quickly learns that crying will usually bring someone to take care of it. The baby also learns that a smile will bring a smile back — and maybe other Warm Fuzzies, too, like being picked up or cuddled. Little girls often learn how to get daddies to laugh and little boys learn how to tease mommy and get her to smile. Of course it works the other way too because getting dad to laugh or teasing mom isn't limited to either sex.

Sometimes the Little Professor just knows things without having learned them. Did anyone ever say to you: "How did you know that?" You replied, "I don't know. I just knew it." That's your LP at work. This ability to know is called intuition. (in-too-i-shun) It's a very useful and helpful part of your Child.

NATURAL CHILD AND LITTLE PROFESSOR — WHO KNOWS WHAT WILL HAPPEN?

Sometimes your NC wants more fun than is good for you or maybe the kind of fun that is dangerous. Your LP comes up with a great invention and NC wants to try it, for fun. For instance: jumping off the roof to try out home-made wings might be fun and exciting for NC and LP — but all three parts of you might get badly hurt if the wings don't work.

So your Parent says: "Don't do it, you'll get hurt." Your thinking Adult says: "It's OK if it works but it may not work so I guess we'd better put a net under you." Your Natural Child says: "I want to fly now." Your Little Professor says: "I dreamt it all up, it'll work, we don't need a net."

What do you suppose happens?

THE ADAPTED CHILD, MAYBE A REBEL, A SULK, OR A JERK!

Your Adapted Child is that part of you which acts in response to other people. If someone is bossy and tells you what to do, what do you do? Do you say NO? If so, you may be in what is called your rebellious Child. The Rebel Kid helps set us apart from other people. The first time we do this is when we're about two years old. Later we may do it when we're sixteen.

Being a rebel is important for your development as a person — but no one needs to rebel all the time. It really gets you and everyone else all tired out!

THE JERK

On the other hand, always saying "yes" and doing what you're asked to do is boring. Maybe you think the only way to get strokes is to be "good" and do everything the way others want you to. Lots of PICs (teachers, mothers, fathers, priests, rabbis, ministers) *do* give strokes only for doing what they ask (passive behavior). So we are taught to please PICs even though other kids may call us teacher's pet, sissy, or baby.

Dr. Berne called people who *always* try to please PICs "Jerks." Jerks may go through their whole lives trying to please PICs (bosses, leaders, mothers, wives, etc.) and never get to do what they want to do. There's nothing wrong with pleasing other people if you *choose* to do this. The OK Adapted Child learns to get along with other people, to be accepted for being polite, to behave in ways that are appropriate at school or home or church. The Not OK Adapted Child is *always* good or obedient without using his Adult to check things out.

THE SULK

Kids who keep quiet and pout are called "Sulks." Sulking is being mad inside and being afraid to say it out loud. Maybe if you can talk about what's bothering you, you won't have to sulk. To stop sulking, take the risk and say what is bothering you, like "I don't like it when you yell at me."

Do you fit any of these? Remember your Child is OK and every one of us has all these parts inside us. Your Adult can help you to know what to do instead of *always* pleasing PICs, *always* rebelling, *always* being good, or *always* pouting or sulking.

Talk about this with your PICs at school or at home and see what they suggest.

35

EXERCISES

Here are some childlike words and actions. How many do you use? You're OK to use them but it's important to know you are in your Child when you do.

No I won't	Whew	Crying
You can't make me	Right on	Laughing
I like you	Ouch	Eating ice cream
Let's go out and play	Oh, no!	Pouting
Let's make believe that...	I want it now	Whining
	Darn	Worrying
I don't know	Heck	Sulking
Please	Gee	Jumping rope
Yippee	Golly	Being afraid
I hate you	Yes, Ma'am	Being sad
Wow	Climbing trees	Being mad
Look at me	Slamming doors	

1. A person who always does what he is asked to do in an effort to please important people is called a _____.
2. The part of the Child which imagines, invents, is sometimes a smarty, but also gets its own way is called the _____.
3. The _____ Child laughs and cries, is angry or happy, has and expresses all kinds of feelings.
4. The Rebel Kid who says NO is part of the _____ Child. (See page 100 for the answers.)

WORDS AND IDEAS FOR YOUR ADULT

Child	Rebel
Adapted Child	Sulk
Little Professor	Jerk
Free or Natural Child	

36

We have met the enemy and they are us.
— Pogo

CHAPTER SIX
How to Know Who's in Charge
Parent, Adult, or Child

We know now the three people or parts inside of us — the Parent, the Adult, and the Child. We know that sometimes one part is in charge and sometimes another. Now, how can we use them to get along better and feel better about ourselves?

When we are kind and are taking care of someone else, our Parent is in charge.

When we are smiling, dreaming, crying, playing, fighting, swearing, or insisting on doing what we want NOW, who's in charge? Our Child? Right. Sometimes in TA we refer to the Child in us as the "Kid."

HOW CAN WE TELL WHO'S IN CHARGE?

If we know who's in charge of us, we can also figure out who's in charge of other people: our friends, teacher, or family. There are four ways to know which Ego State (P-A-C) is in charge. In TA we ask ourselves, "Where am I coming from, my P, A, or C?"

First, you *know how you feel*. Do you feel angry, hurt, sad, afraid, happy, loving? Your Child is the part of you where your feelings are — so when your feelings are strong and in control of you, your C is in charge. An interesting thing, though — when you start *thinking about* your feelings, your A takes over.

THE WORDS YOU USE

Second, *by your language*. Ow! Oops! Neat! Yuk! Wow! If you're sounding off with words like those above or if you're laughing or giggling, you're in your Kid.

38

We have already talked about this a little in Chapters Three, Four, and Five but here are three lists of words for you to check. When you hear yourself or someone else using words like these, then you can tell whether your P, A, or C is turned on.

Parent	Adult	Child
That's a no-no	Better	Wow
Stop that!	Easier	Yummy
Ridiculous!	I think so	Heck
That's stupid	I can figure it out	Pow
Silly	I'm going to study now	The greatest
Shame on you	That's a help	The pits! (or other
Let me help you	Will you help me,	slang)
Think positive	please	Cool
Let me worry about it	May I have an apple	I want
Keep a stiff upper lip	No thanks, I'd rather	I don't want
Turn that frown	walk	Darn (or worse)
upside down	The answer is 98	
Go to your room	The school is three	
I love you very much	blocks from here	
You're pretty sharp		

BY THE WAY THEY ACT TOWARDS YOU

A third way to know who is in charge is to *be aware of how other people are acting toward you.* If you see lots of Parent in others' reactions to you, you can bet that your C is "hooking"* them. And if the P is coming on strong, you'll probably see the Child in the other person.

If you yell at your little brother or sister: "You get off my bed," what will he/she say? Well, whatever it is, I'll bet it is a C answer.

*Hook means to turn on or stroke.

BY THE WAY YOU ACT

You can also figure out who's in charge *by the way you act*. This is the fourth way. Are you screaming, crying, whining, throwing a temper tantrum, day-dreaming, giving a Warm Fuzzy, laughing? That is your Child. Sometimes you do something impulsively (without planning) just because you want to. That's your Child too.

Are you scolding, shaking your finger at someone, putting a band-aid on your sister's skinned knee, spanking your dog, helping your brother fix his skate board? You've probably seen your mother or father do these things — so your P acts that way too.

If you are reading this book and answering the questions, if you are trying to figure out who's in charge of you, if you answer the telephone and take a message, your A is in charge at that point.

WHY BOTHER?

Why is it important to know all this? Because if I can find out which one of me is boss, I can have a lot more fun, make more sense, and get along better with people around me. Sometimes when I talk to people, they don't seem to listen. Sometimes I don't hear what they are saying to me. Maybe that is because the ME they are talking to is turned off. So then maybe I can talk in a different way (from my A instead of my P) and we can talk and understand each other.

CONTAMINATION

Oh yes, there's one other thing we wanted to talk about. Sometimes one of the three people inside us gets messed up by the others. It is as if we put our fingers in our ears and can't hear. This happens when one of the people, like the Child or Parent, is very much in charge and we don't want to hear anything else.

If the Child hears what mother has to say, the Child will have to stop what it's doing. For example, more than once when I was deep into a book, mother would say, "Will you please get up and go to the store for me" (or something else I didn't want to do). My Child didn't want to hear that so I would say "Uh huh" and keep on reading. Later when she would get angry, I would wonder what all the heat was about. Since my Child had shut out her earlier request, I didn't remember it.

41

This messing up of the Adult so that the message doesn't get through is called a big word that you don't have to remember unless you want to. It's called contamination. You can say it if you can read it, contamination. All it means is "messed up." Like smeared with mud so that you can't really see the person. But that "messing up" sometimes messes up the way we learn to talk to each other.

If we are angry, our Adult is messed up so we can't really hear what you're saying. Maybe you were asking if we'd like some ice cream! We may say something out of our childlike anger that has nothing to do with your question. That's why sometimes we have to take a look and find out what our Kid is doing. Sometimes it messes up all of the fun we can have with other people.

LEARNING IS AN ADULT ACTIVITY

We have been learning some new things about ourselves. We know that there are three people inside of us. We call them "Parent," "Adult," and "Child." These three people are very real. They express our feelings, the bossy and caring part of us, and the part that makes sense. Any one of them can be messed up or knocked out by any one of the others. When that happens, we can't hear what other people are saying to us. Then we use what we feel or what we believe to make our decisions. This means that we can't understand other people nor they us. That's what gets us into trouble. In the rest of the chapters of this book we'll try to find out how to do better than that so that we're happier every day.

EXERCISES

Now let's see if you can tell when A, C, or P is talking:

1. I hurt my toes, darn it. _____

2. I'll put some medicine and a Band-Aid on it. _____

3. That was a stupid thing I did, kicking that can. _____

If you labeled #1 — C, #2 — A, and #3 — P, you've been strengthening your A while you read. Number 1 was expressing feelings and Number 3 was Critical Parent while Number 2 was thinking and planning.

1. Name the one inside of you who thinks for yourself. _____

2. Name the one inside of you who makes sense. _____

3. You can make a computer but a computer cannot make you. True or false. _____

4. A takes care of C by thinking. True or false. _____

5. Only your A makes decisions based on fact. True or false. _____

6. P works like a cash register. True or false. _____

7. A works like a tape recorder. True or false. _____

The answers are on page 100.

SOME WORDS AND IDEAS FOR YOUR ADULT

Contamination

"Coming on from"

Messing up the Adult

"OK" means adequate, worthwhile, important.
— Thomas A. Harris

CHAPTER SEVEN
I'm OK — You're OK

In Chapter II we talked a great deal about strokes. We learned that strokes are very important. If we don't get them when we're little, we get unhappy, may get sick or even die. At first we got them just for being. Later we learned that plus strokes are often given to us for things that we do right. We get the feeling that we have to earn them and only deserve them if we do something well. Strokes are often given for doing (or not doing) what very important people, known as mother and dad, want us to do or to avoid doing. We like it when people give us strokes just because we're us. We wish they would give them to us more often for that reason. Do you ever feel that way? That you would like to have strokes just because you're you, and not because of what you do? Or know? Or how pretty or handsome you are?

WHAT OK MEANS:

Warm Fuzzies (the plus strokes) make people feel good, feel OK. "OK" means "worth something, able, and important." You're able to think, you are important to yourself and others, and you are worth a great deal just because you are a person. Do you feel you are OK? Yes? No? How did you get that feeling? How did you get a feeling of not OK? Talk about that now. How can you change from feeling not OK to feeling OK?

EVERYBODY IS BORN OK (AND YOU STILL ARE)

When you were born you were OK. *Everbody is OK when they are born* (worthwhile, able and important). You were worth more than anything else in the world to your mother and father or to someone who cared for you, but if they didn't there are lots of us who would have if we'd known you then. But ask your mother or father how much they would sell you for. And while they may tease a little and say: "Make me an offer," they wouldn't take any amount, not even a million billion dollars, for you. So you have worth, not just alone in money, although that's important, but you have worth just because you exist. Oh, I know they will tell you sometimes, "Go get lost," or even "Go and play on the freeway," but they don't mean it because you *are* important. You are a part of them. You count.

Some people are not always welcome by their mother and father when they arrive here. They are "given up for adoption." That doesn't change their value or their OKness. It merely means the natural mother or father wasn't ready to love a baby or to take care of it. Other caring people took the baby and loved it.

Being "able" means able to think. There isn't one of you who isn't able to think enough to do what's required of you. You're OK means being worthwhile, being important to yourself and others, and being able to do what you need to do. Everybody, and I mean *everybody*, is born OK. How come, then, that so many of us often have feelings of being not OK? Well, here's the way it goes.

HOW I CHANGED FROM A PRINZ INTO A FROZ (Not OK Feelings)

PRINZES   FROZZES

When you are first born, you're OK and you feel OK. You feel like a Prinz (Prince or Princess). Later you get Cold Pricklies that cause you to lose your OK feelings and to begin to feel like a Froz (a boy or girl frog). Most mothers and fathers take good care of you, give you strokes, love you and hold you close, and so on. If you hadn't gotten strokes then, you wouldn't be here to read this book. Then you start to grow and they feel they must teach you what to do to be "human." So they start giving you strokes for doing what they want you to do.

Now suppose it happens that you're not able to do what they want you to do when they want you to do it or in the way that they want you to do it. (Sounds like a song.) Then they tell you what's wrong or how bad you are or how nasty and mean and ugly and disobedient (that's a big word) or how uncooperative you are (that's another big word that you may not understand).

Then at the ripe age of two you may say to yourself in two-year-old words: "Wow, what a mess I am. Nobody loves me. Nothing I do pleases anybody. I am just a failure. You know what, I couldn't have gotten this way by myself in this short space of time. It must be that I was born a mess, a failure. I guess I am a defective product. I'm not really OK and I never will be. I'm a born loser."

Then you may continue, "Mother and dad know how to do everything right. They are big and smart and I am little and stupid. *So they and everybody else* are OK. They're all important, worthwhile and, adequate, but not me. I'm not OK. They are OK." Boy, that's a tough position to be in.

47

Suddenly you realize that if you're not OK, you won't get strokes. And you *need* strokes. You are scared because "If I'm not OK, nobody will love me, nobody will give me strokes and I'll *die*." So you've got to do something to take care of that. And then you make a big decision at the age of two or three. "Even though I'm not OK, I won't let anybody else know it. I'll *keep a nice smile on my face* and I'll be good and do what they want me to. That way they'll give me strokes and think I'm OK even though *I know I'm not*." Someday when I meet a prince or princess, he or she will know my true worth and I'll get my OK back."

AN EARLY DECISION

That decision, which you and I made a long time ago, is keeping us from feeling OK now. That little kid, two years old, made a decision that you and I are still believing. We're still letting that little child run our lives. Isn't that silly of us?

What are some of the not OK feelings you have? How can we get rid of them? How can we change from frogs or ugly ducklings into the prince or princess that we really are?

Of course, being OK doesn't mean that everything we do is perfect or even "right." Lots of times you and I make mistakes and we don't always please ourselves or other people. But that doesn't change the fact that I'm OK and so are you and so are they.

Remember — "YOU ARE OK." Say it, "I'm OK and You're OK" and that's the truth. There is no doubt about it.

EXERCISES

1. Decide if you are OK.

2. Decide if you agree that everyone is OK. If not, find out why in this book we believe it is true. Talk about it with your teacher or other PIC.

3. Are you a Froz or a Prinz? Want to change?

WORDS AND IDEAS FOR YOUR ADULT

Adequate

Worthwhile

Important

OK

Froz and Prinz

I'm not OK — you're OK

I'm OK — You're OK

CHAPTER EIGHT
Stamp Collections

Does your family save Green Stamps or Blue Chip Stamps? We used to. What do you do with them? That's right, you stick them in a book until it is full and then you can get something good that you want for free.

Our Child likes to put Blue Chip Stamps in a book and dream about what they'll bring when the book is full. (Boy, maybe we'll get a motorcycle.) Our Parent likes this, too, because we believe we are saving money, even if our Adult says we're not.

TA BROWN STAMPS

The Child in us collects another kind of stamp. We'll call these TA Brown Stamps. Whenever we get our feelings hurt, get afraid, or get mad, we may keep those mean feelings inside. Then we are saving TA Brown Stamps.

Saving Brown Stamps means saving up feelings to trade in later for strokes that we feel we've got coming to us. Just like when we trade in the Blue Chip Stamps, we get a free prize. If we save enough anger, sometime we're going to have a temper tantrum or a fight (anger without feeling guilty is the "free prize"). Maybe that will happen when we least expect it over some little thing that really doesn't mean anything. Did that ever happen to you? It's sort of like putting in one more stamp to fill the book and then you can get your free prize all at once.

Some people use different colors to talk about different kinds of saved up feelings (red for anger, blue for fear, brown for NOT OK). Lately though, TA people use "brown" stamps to include all these saved-up feelings. Also when someone gives you a compliment (a stroke) and you don't accept it, we say you're painting the gold stamp "brown."

The secret of Brown Stamps is that they are printed inside us. When P calls C "stupid" the Child prints a Brown Stamp and that's a saved stroke. Then we either throw it away or put it in a stamp book for a "gotcha"* later.

TODAY I COLLECTED BROWN STAMPS

Here is a story of how I might get some Brown Stamps. I am on my way to school and I see John, who is a friend of mine, walking with a girl who is a friend of his. So I say to him, "Hi, John," and John walks right on by and doesn't say anything.

*"Now we got you" for doing a mean thing to us earlier.

I think I have strokes coming to me from John so I put two Brown Stamps in my "feeling" book. Later on in class Mary leans over and asks for a pencil. I start to tell her that I do not have one. The teacher sees me and bawls me out for speaking during class. I don't say anything, but I put away another Brown Stamp. That was so unfair to get blamed and not be able to tell anyone.

Later on somebody at home asks me to do something: turn off the TV or run an errand. Then I explode all over the place about how everybody picks on me and nobody likes me, all they want to do is use me and so on. Everbody wonders why I am so upset. Of

course, I don't remember to tell them about John and Mary. All I do is unload on them because it's safer at home. So you can say that I traded in my Brown Stamps for a big temper tantrum at home. Some prize, a temper tantrum — felt good to let it out but everybody else felt bad.

WHAT TO DO WITH BROWN STAMPS

Our C can do three things with Brown Stamps. We can keep them and save them up for a big explosion, throw them away as soon as they are printed, or not print them at all.

The only way that somebody can give you Brown Stamps, "make you angry" is when your Parent agrees with them and your Adult doesn't stop the Brown Stamp printing machine. OK? Well, your Adult can throw Brown Stamps away. Or your C can say, "Hey, John, I spoke to you, didn't you hear me?" Or A can say, "Well, maybe John doesn't want to talk to me now. He's busy talking with Wendy. I'll see him later. I don't have to worry about it or be hurt."

Later on when I think about Mary and what happened, I can say to myself, "Well, I can protect Mary. Really, it's not going to hurt anybody and I guess the teacher's kind of upset about the noise in the room, so I'll just keep quiet and forget it. I'm OK and she's OK." Later on if I have picked up any stamps, I can talk about it to Mary. I'll tell her how mad I got when it happened, that I'm not angry with her and guess the teacher had a right to tell me about it.

Thus Brown Stamps can be printed or not printed. Brown Stamps can be saved or thrown away. Do you have any today? Talk about them to someone. Maybe they can tell you how you can go about getting rid of them.

EXERCISES

1. a. Write a story about how you might collect some Brown Stamps; when you feel angry, hurt, worried, helpless, afraid — and didn't do anything except save up your feelings.
   b. Now tell how you could have avoided collecting Brown Stamps.

2. Act out your story with two or three others in your class. See if you can end the story with a way to get rid of your stamp collection.

3. Make a "stamp box" for school or home where you can throw away any Brown Stamps you collect. Plan a time when you can have a ceremony to empty the box.

4. Tell the person whom you're unhappy with about what he or she did and why you didn't like it. Then forget it.

WORDS AND IDEAS FOR YOUR ADULT

Blue Chip Stamps

TA Brown Stamps

Free prize

CHAPTER NINE
Transactions

HOW YOU AND I TALK TO EACH OTHER

A transaction is the giving and taking of a stroke. It's the way people talk to each other. It's the way they send and receive messages and the way they give and take Warm Fuzzies or Cold Pricklies. Remember in Chapter Two, the arrows for strokes 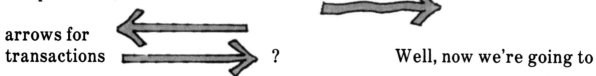 and the arrows for transactions ? Well, now we're going to talk a little more about these double arrows — transactions. A transaction has two strokes. One is the stimulus stroke which makes you "feel." The other stroke is the answer to the first stroke which we call a response stroke.

A PARALLEL TRANSACTION

If I ask you "What time is it?", that is an Adult question. Right? It looks like this:

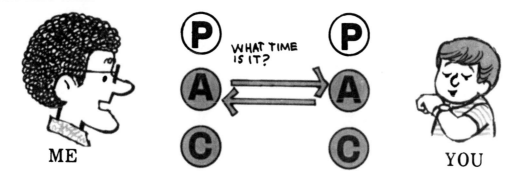

ME   YOU

1. This is a stimulus stroke.

If you answer, "It is ten o'clock" — that is a factual answer, from your A, and it looks like this:

2.   ME   YOU

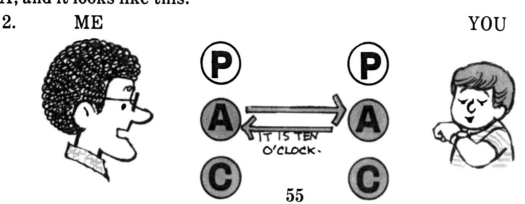

Both together like this makes a transaction:

3.

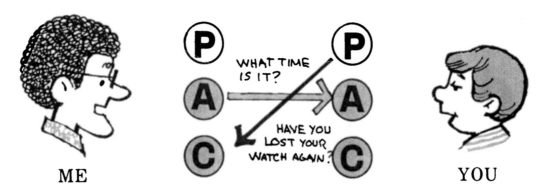

Now you have a picture of a straight or parallel transaction. The lines of the strokes are parallel and information is clear. We'll probably keep on talking.

A CROSSED TRANSACTION

You might answer me in a different way, though. If when I asked you, "What time is it?" and you had replied with the question, "Have you lost your watch again?" that would be your P talking to my C. The transaction would look like this:

See how the lines cross? That is a crossed transaction and we are no longer communicating. In fact, we probably have a series of unpleasant transactions or even an argument.

56

Again, your C might answer the question. You might say something like this: "It's half past time to go out and play." Here's another crossed transaction from your C to my P.

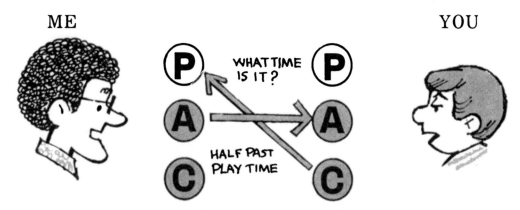

ME   YOU

Again we lose our communication.

Straight transactions come and go from

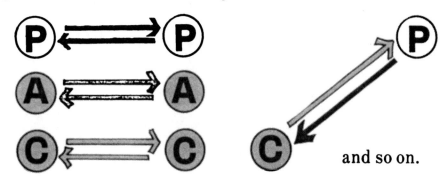

and so on.

So long as the lines don't cross, are parallel, we'll continue to speak to each other. If they cross, we'll either stop talking or have a fight.

Why do we need to know about transactions? Well, maybe you have wondered why someone gets mad at you when you ask a simple question. The answer may be because your transactions were crossed — and neither of you knew it. Of course you don't like it when people are angry with you.

EARLY TRANSACTIONS

When you were little, the first transactions you had with mother and dad formed your Child and your Parent. Every transaction you have ever had then or since was recorded on your brain and you never forgot it. If you wanted to, you could remember whatever happened to you from the time you were a tiny baby. The very important and painful transactions we tend to remember easily. Like the time I stuck my finger into the open electric outlet. How frightened I was when I got a shock! Or the time Mother told me I must *share* two chocolate cookies with my cousin Leonard and I didn't want to. I remember that because the whole thing was so unpleasant.

We remember the feelings but we often can't remember what it was all about. Somebody says, "I got a spanking one time. Boy! I'll never forget it." And I say, "What was it for?" They reply, "Oh, I don't know. Something I did." We remember the spanking but we don't remember the reason.

DOUBLE TRANSACTIONS (Duplex)

Sometimes a transaction is hidden. We say one thing but mean something else at the same time. For example, you may say to your sister while grownups are busy talking, "Hey, sis, let's go out and play in the yard." And your sister says, "Okay, let's go."

Really what you are saying is, "Hey, sis, these grownups are boring, let's get away from them." And sister knows what you mean and says, "Okay, let's." If you were to draw a diagram, it would look like this:

Sometimes double transactions happen without our knowing it. Then it's a hidden transaction and a series of these is a Game.

The most important transaction is the parallel one. The reason that this kind of transaction is important is because it's the one that helps us to make sense and to understand ourselves and other people. Not all transactions are verbal. Gestures, salutes, frowns and smiles, touches and other physical strokes are ways of transacting.

EXERCISES FOR GROUP

Let's see how many different kinds of verbal transactions we can think up and write down. What are some you had today in school, at home, out on the playground? Can you tell the difference between a parallel, a cross, and a double transaction? Write an example of each. Draw the diagrams and see if you can make them clear to yourself and other people with the use of lines and circles. You'll find that it is a lot of fun to figure out who is saying what to whom, and what they mean by it. If you can't figure it out and you get stuck, bring it in to class or ask someone at home to help you figure it out.

Here are some first lines. You fill in the second; check page 100 when you are finished.

1. When you say, "Hello," to someone you are giving them a _____ _____.

2. When you speak to someone from your A to their A and they answer you the same way you have a _____ transaction.

3. When you speak to the A in someone and they answer from their C you have a _____ transaction.

4. When a cross transaction happens you're most likely to have a _____.

5. When two people speak at one level (like from A to A) but mean something else (like from C to C) they are having a _____ transaction.

6. Make up a story to show how someone can answer the same question from their P or A or C.

WORDS AND IDEAS FOR YOUR ADULT

Transactions

Complementary (parallel) transactions

Crossed transactions

Duplex (ulterior or hidden) transactions

CHAPTER TEN
Games We All Play

FUN IS IMPORTANT

What fun games do you enjoy the most? Do you like hopscotch, baseball, hockey, jump rope, Yahtze, Old Maid, checkers, Marco Polo (in the water) or what? Most people, young or old, like to play games for fun.

Some boys and girls like to play with dolls and make believe they are keeping house like their mothers and fathers. Others like running games or climbing. Some people love to build models and as they get older (and richer) the models get bigger and more expensive.

Doing things for fun is very important for everyone. If your folks like to play tennis, swim, hike, go bowling, play cards or ride bikes, life is probably better for you, too. Because when folks are happy, home is a nice place to be.

Fun games are a good way of getting strokes, especially when you win. It feels good to win, but if you have to win to be happy, maybe you're not getting enough free Warm Fuzzies. Playing is also a way to keep your Child from being bored. You become bored when your Kid is not getting any strokes. Dullsville. So fun games get you strokes and help you to feel OK. I suggest two hours of fun for everyone, every day, to stay healthy.

TA GAMES ARE NOT THE SAME

TA Games are different from fun games. While we play TA games to get strokes, there is at least one major difference — when you play a TA game, you don't know you are playing, or even why. Wow! How can that be?

In order to help you to understand what I just said, I'd like to explain a TA game. Often when something is being said, something else is meant. Eric Berne first told about TA Games. According to him, a TA Game is a series of transactions (between two or more people) which lead to a payoff or a prize. The strokes are parallel — that is, if a person speaks from his Parent to your Child, your Child will respond to his Parent. That would look like this:

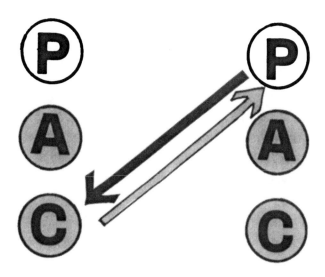

Then the Parent would respond, then the Child and so on.

The difference between an ordinary conversation and a TA Game is that while the transactions seem straight and open, there is really something else going on.

Berne calls this something else "transactions of an *ulterior* nature." "Ulterior" means hidden or sneaky, or for a different purpose than what is being said. Actually there are two sets of transactions going on at the same time — what is being said and what is meant.

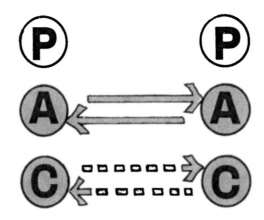

A TA Game is usually played over and over, and it begins, continues, and ends the same way. Have you ever heard something start at your house and you could predict the way it would end — with somebody in tears and somebody else angry or hurt?

The end of the Game is called the payoff. Payoffs are the real purpose of the Game. We play Games because we're afraid to ask for what we want or because we're afraid to change but think we should. *Games are crooked ways of getting strokes*, played by the Child, usually without the knowledge of the Adult. That's why I said we don't even know we are playing. When someone else tells us we *are* playing a Game, we usually deny it and tell them why what we are saying or doing is perfectly right and why the other person is wrong.

THE FIRST GAME

The Game that most people play first — at a very young age — is called "Mine's better than yours." We play it to get strokes when we don't think we can get strokes just for being. So in order to get them, we try to convince other people that we should be rewarded.

"TATTLETALE"

"Tattle-tale" is a relative of "Mine's better." Have you ever played either of these? Here's a drawing, using P, A, and C and stroke arrows to explain what a Game looks like:

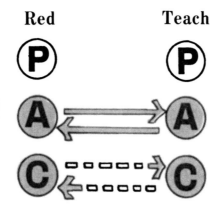

Red   Teach

1. "Teach! Cheri left the schoolyard."
2. "Teach, give me some strokes for telling you and for obeying you. Your fear tells me you like me to tell you."

Payoff for Red

1. "She did?" (shock)
2. "I'm frightened! People will blame me if she gets lost!
   "Thanks, Red, I'll punish her and *reward* you. I can *depend* on Red.

Payoff for Teach

65

You probably noticed that there are two sets of arrows. We call the ones in the Adult, the ones you can see or hear, the Social level, while the hidden ones at the Child level are called the Psychological strokes. These are the hidden or ulterior strokes and are what Games are all about.

"WHY DON'T YOU — YES BUT"

Another Game that you often hear people playing is called "What should I do — Why Don't You — YES BUT!" If you listen to people speaking, you'll hear the Game. It may sound like this:

Cheri: What should I do about my brothers? They're always taking my money, cake, handkerchiefs (or something).

Counselor: Well, why don't you share your things with them?

Cheri: Well, YES BUT they won't share with me.

Mike: Well, you could agree that they can take your things if you can take theirs.

Cheri: YES, BUT they don't *have* anything I want. And besides they won't let me use their things.

David: Well, you could put a lock on your door.

Cheri: YES, BUT my mother won't let me and besides locks cost money.

So the games goes on until the counselor and the other people give up. No one says anything and then they talk about something else. When Cheri leaves she says to herself, "See, there's no way to solve my problem. No one knows the answer. I showed them they're not so smart." The counselor can say "Look how hard we tried to help Cheri." Each gets some satisfaction out of the Game.

THESE TWO GO ON AT THE SAME TIME

Social level: what is said   Game (hidden) level: What is meant

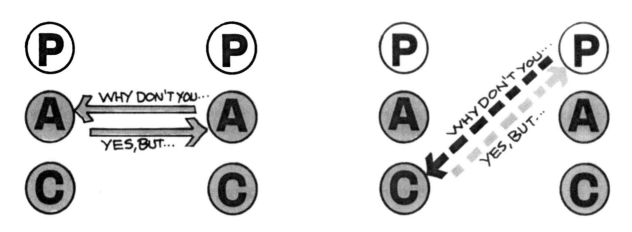

REPEATED AGAIN AND AGAIN

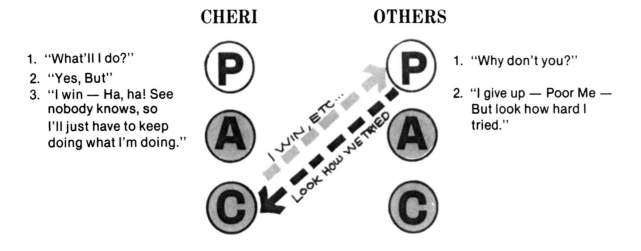

PAY OFF

CHERI   **OTHERS**

1. "What'll I do?"
2. "Yes, But"
3. "I win — Ha, ha! See nobody knows, so I'll just have to keep doing what I'm doing."

1. "Why don't you?"

2. "I give up — Poor Me — But look how hard I tried."

THE GAME PLAN*

To figure out if you are playing TA Games, ask yourself the following set of questions:

1. What keeps happening to me over and over that leaves me or someone else feeling bad?
2. What happens next?
3. And then what happens?
4. How does it end?
5. How do I feel after it ends?
6. How might the other person feel?

If you want to avoid the Payoff of the Game — stop the game as soon as you recognize you're getting into the same old thing. Then ask for what you want — strokes.

One way to do that is to follow the next set of ideas. Say:

When you _____
          (do or say things like that)

I get _____
     (angry, hurt or afraid)

So I would like you to _____
                      (stop, do something else, and so on)

If you decide not to play a Game, the first step is to recognize the beginning of it. Berne calls this the Hook. "What shall I do?" is the Hook in the second Game we mentioned. If you avoid giving advice, you won't get into the Game. Another Game avoider is to give the person strokes. Like: "I'm sure that you will figure it out — you're pretty smart."

*John James, The Game Plan, TA Journal 3:4:73

NAME A GAME

Oh, yes, by the way — avoid naming other people's Games. You'll only make them mad. People who play NAG (name-a-game) aren't too well liked.

It's like pulling the covers off someone to wake them up in the morning. You're "trying to help them" but they won't thank you. So just avoid playing the Game when you recognize a Hook. Your payoff then will be better feelings for you and for them.

OTHER GAMES PEOPLE PLAY

Here are some names of other famous *Games People Play* from Eric Berne's book by the same name. How many of them do you recognize? The names of the Games are either what the Game begins with or usually ends with, like:

"See what you made me do"   "Wooden leg" (wooden head)
"If it weren't for you"   "Uproar"
"Now I've got you"   "Let's you and him fight"
"Kick me"   "Blemish"
"Stupid"

and a whole lot of others and most of all "Cops and Robbers." These Games are described in several other books; ask your teacher or some other PIC to go over them with you.

EXERCISES

1. Why is playing Games undesirable? By the way, can you tell who is playing these Games (P, A, or C) from the title? Label them now and see if you agree with others in the group. Tell why you thought they were P, A, or C playing.

2. Make up a play to show how "Why don't you, Yes But" is played in the classroom between a pupil and teacher.

3. What is John James' Game Plan? How could you use it?

4. Try this when someone does something you don't like:
   a. When you _____
       (do what I don't like)
   b. I feel _____
       (sad, angry or hurt)
   c. And I want you to _____
       (stop, do something else)
(Practice this in class or at home)

5. Try the opposite, too, to tell people when you *like* what they are doing.

WORDS AND IDEAS FOR YOUR ADULT

The Game — define it — learn what

   it means

"Mine's Better Than Yours"

The Game Plan

Formula for being straight

If you want to feel different, change what you are doing.
— Alvyn M. Freed

CHAPTER ELEVEN
TA Rackets

In the last chapter we talked about Games. Many other books (*Games People Play, Games Students Play* and so on) have been written about TA Games. Now we're going to talk about Rackets because TA Games grow out of Rackets.

The word Racket is borrowed from gangster talk. A gangster is working a "protection racket" when he forces a storekeeper, for instance, to keep quiet. In other words, "Don't make a racket or tell the police or scream for help." The racketeer uses threats, anger, or violence to force the victim to *keep his feelings in* and to pay him not to hurt him, break up his store, injure his family, or do other mean things to him.

The racketeer (gangster) *acts* angry and covers his excitement. On the other hand the victim feels fear and anger but keeps quiet and pays money or goods for the so-called protection. Both are covering their real feelings.

TA Rackets are like this. Sometimes people who were very hurt when they were young, go around all of their lives acting angry. They tell me "I'm even-tempered — always mad" (that's a joke, I think). In fact, without knowing it, TA Racketeers look for people (victims) to talk to, who will not feel sympathy for their old hurt, so they can again feel hurt and rejected — like they did when they were young. We say they are working their anger Racket when they do this.

AN ANGER RACKET

Here's an example: Marcia came in the other day and, after a series of transactions, began saying the same thing she has said many times before:

"You always blame me"
"You never blame my sister"
"I'm angry (hurt) at you"
"I give up trying to convince you"
"I'm leaving"

Then she leaves in anger. She feels hurt, rejected, defeated (but secure, safe, and right). Here is a clear case of an anger Racket. When Marcia was young, her family yelled and screamed a lot. That was what home was to her. The fights scared her and she still feels scared when others fight, but her feelings of safety increase when she is fighting. Thus families teach Rackets.

RACKETS BRING BACK OLD FEELINGS

Mom may be working a Racket when she says, "I'll be frightened or worried if you don't call me. Write to me every day while you're in camp." When you do write or call, she again feels she is being loved — like when she was little. So she uses a Racket to get love. Perhaps she doesn't get enough love to keep her happy.

Fathers sometimes use anger to get and keep control of the family and thus feel safe themselves. They force obedience, feel proud and safe (old feelings) when everything is under control. Sometimes their sons or daughters act bossy and tough in the same way. They've learned a Racket.

Are you a Racketeer? What kind? How do you feel when someone does it to you? Do you like them? If not and you want to avoid turning people off, turn your Adult on (start thinking with facts) and see if you are working a Racket.

SOME FAMILY RACKETS

Does your family have a Racket? Here are some I've heard of:

> "You'll make me nervous if you —"
> "You know when you do *that* I get worried."
> "You've done it again — now I'll be depressed all day."
> "Do it again and we won't go on the trip."
> "Don't bother about me, I'll be all right."
> "You know I can't stand a messy kitchen."

Rackets lead to Games. Games like IIWFY*, Poor Me, Kick Me, NIGY** (refer to Chapter Ten) all stem from a yearning to re-experience feelings you had when you were *very* young. One way to know it's a Racket or a Game is to ask yourself if this same thing has happened before. If it has, you are probably following a series of moves which lead to the same old feeling. To avoid this, recognize it and change the pattern — in other words, don't do the same thing if you want different results.

EXERCISES

Now here's a little quiz for you whiz kids. Not that you'll need them, but the answers are at the end of this book.

1. Racket is a family's way of getting strokes. True or false.

2. Boys and girls learn the family Racket in school. True or false.

3. Kids can learn to collect "happy" stamps if they're shown how by their family. True or false.

WORDS AND IDEAS FOR YOUR ADULT

TA Racket

Protection Racket

Family Rackets

*If It Wasn't For You   **Now I've Got You

CHAPTER TWELVE
Scripts

WHEN YOU GET BIG

"What are you going to be if the neighbors let you grow up, Dennis?"* Has anyone ever said things like this to you:

"When you grow up, you'll make a great nurse." (or doctor, wife, father, mechanic, teacher, crook).

"If you keep that up, you'll wind up a jailbird."

"If you're not careful, young lady, you'll grow up to be like your Aunt Dirty Myrty, a no good."

Maybe you feel mixed up if you've heard people say things like that. You may now have the idea that no matter what you do, you'll wind up as they said you would. You may feel that your life was all planned out for you before you were born, that there is nothing you can do to change it.

*From the cartoon by the same name.

75

NOBODY IS FATED!

Each of us can make a choice or even many choices in our lives. We can change our whole life plan, whenever we decide to do so. We can do it more than once, too.

Mother told me when I was eight years old that I was a natural salesman. I spent several years after High School trying to be a successful salesman, without success. Then she convinced me to be a teacher and I did all right but got bored with it. Some of her plans I carried out and some I didn't. And I changed everything several times. Then on my own I decided to study psychology. Now I am an author, a publisher, and a psychologist. Marge, who is helping me rewrite this book, and who has written two other fine books, once wanted to be a newspaper woman. Later she became a dancer and a great teacher. So you see you know at least two people who got out of their scripts and did what they could do best.

SCRIPTY MESSAGES

Those statements at the beginning of this chapter are called "Scripty messages." If you follow them, it's like your life is a stage play. You see, the *story* of a play or a movie is called a script. Since the end of the play is planned before the play begins, if you are acting in it, you cannot change how it ends. This is, you can't change, you must say your lines just as they are written so that the play goes as planned. If you accept someone else's Script for your life, you're pretty much in the same place. You feel you must follow their Script. Of course you need not.

Scripty messages have been called "self fulfilling prophecies" — that's a mouthful for you. If you accept what someone else predicts that you will do or be, then you will be making that prophecy come true. It's sort of like your *fate* has been decided for you by someone else. By following a Script you needn't make decisions for yourself.

YOU CAN CHANGE

Well, to the best of my knowledge, you can change the plan *whenever you choose to do so.* First, of course you must be aware of what Scripty messages you received when you were young. Next, find out what you are doing to make your Script work. If you are playing some TA Games, you can knock off the Games and start coming on straight. You can move straight towards your goal in life, not a goal someone else laid on you. The choice is yours: you can decide to follow someone else's Script or your own. If *you choose* to do what you want from your Adult, you can follow your plan or change it at any time of your life.

SAMPLES OF SCRIPTY MESSAGES — How Others Help Script Us

Some boys and girls have older brothers and sisters, who either do very well in school or very badly. Later when the younger person gets into a class with the same teacher, the teacher may give them a Scripty message like this:

"You're *just like* your older brother — a lazy good-for-nothing."

"I remember your older sister, she was good at art, I know *you'll be good* at it too."

"Oh, you're one of the John Dickinson family. *None of you do very well* in school — so you just do your best, but I *won't expect* too *much.*"

"Oh, yes, your brother Klyce was such a good student so I know *you will be too.*"

These are all Scripty messages (the words in *italic*). You can decide not to follow any of them, but to be you.

Of course, if, at home, mother and dad and older brothers and sisters place little value on school work, or doing what teacher says, or attending regularly, or on time — then you may be Scripted before you ever get to school. But it's up to you. You're OK. You can be the kind of student you choose to be.

LOSERS CAN CHANGE TO WINNERS — RIGHT NOW!

Loser Scripts learned early can influence your whole life. *No one needs* to be a loser since we all start out OK. But if you feel Not OK, feel like a loser, and are expected to fail, you probably will. But you can win whenever you decide to do so. Give up feeling and believing in your loser's fate. You're not a loser unless you choose to be.

Now don't misunderstand me: to win, to succeed, takes work, study, practice, and most of all, courage and hanging in there even though you didn't win at first.

King Alfred's story of the spider, which tried six times to spin a web and made it only on the seventh try, inspired him to go back and try again to win his life battle, which he did.

Remember quitters never win and winners never quit. I think quitters are Scripted losers. Which are you, a winner or a loser? If you've been a loser up until now, you can change. Will you? You're OK!

EXERCISES

1. Look up and read the story of King Alfred and the Spider.

2. Do a Script check list to find out:
    a. who is your favorite hero or heroine in a story, in a book, on stage, TV?
    b. what do people predict you will be (if the neighbors let you grow up) or do? (President? Jailbird?)
    c. what do you want to do when you go to work full time, after school ends?
    d. who does your family say you look like, act like? Why? (Dad, Uncle Bilge, Aunty Bulge)
    e. Do they tell you you're shy, too fat, skinny, nervous, quiet, good, bad, weak, strong? How does that fit with the way you see yourself? Want to change? What can you do?

WORDS AND IDEAS FOR YOUR ADULT

Scripts
Scripty messages
Prophecy
Fate
Story of King Alfred
Quitters
Winners

CHAPTER THIRTEEN
People Poisons (PPs) and Antidotes

Did the doctor ever give you a shot? Ouch! Hurts, doesn't it? (And why do they always do it *there*?) Well, now we're going to talk about taking TA SHOTS to prevent NOK (Not OK) which is caused by People Poison (PP). Medical doctors give shots to keep you from getting sick. For example, they give vaccinations against smallpox, polio, and other sicknesses caused by a virus. TA can be thought of as a shot which fights off People Poisons and can protect us from the dreaded NOK disease.

People Poisons are the words People in Charge, and People Less in Charge, like monitors, older brothers and sisters, or baby sitters, sometimes use. These result in our getting the "Not OK" (NOK) disease. They use them to get their own way or to stop us from doing something. They believe that they are protecting us. People Less in Charge are also some of the big kids we play with who bully, call names, act tough, put us down. They're great People Poisoners, too. So watch who you play with and if they send some Poison, you can ignore it.

Somehow we get NOK disease. NOK feels like "I'm no good," "I'm a rotten kid," "I'll never be any good." None of this is true, so forget it.

NOK CARRIERS

Once we accept this dread NOK disease we become carriers and go around giving it to other people like smaller brothers and sisters, friends, or later on, maybe our own children.

No one means to give someone else the NOK disease. You don't and your mother and father didn't. They love you. My mother and dad loved me. But they got the "Not OK" disease from their folks and gave it to me without knowing it. The kids in our neighborhood helped too.

Now we TA'ers know how to stop NOK, how to get rid of it and how to prevent its spread. Wouldn't it be great if no one ever had the NOK disease again? Then everyone would feel so good — like a Prinz all the time. You can help prevent it. You can get rid of your own NOK and never give it to anyone else again if you learn Transactional Analysis, the Warm Fuzzy treatment. Here's how.

THE NOK DISEASE

People with NOK go around feeling Not OK. I guess we all feel that way some of the time. We may be sad, angry, or hurt and not know why. We often carry Brown Stamps around looking for someone or something to dump them on. Some people even dump them on themselves. I know a girl who was so full of Brown Stamps she used to pull her hair out. How come? Well, one of her PP's was, "Don't you dare show your temper to me. Keep it to yourself." So when she got angry she turned it on herself and pulled her hair out, one hair at a time. She looked awful and felt worse. And so did the people who loved her.

81

Another person I know once got so angry at his dad that he set fire to a neighbor's car. He didn't want to hurt anyone but he wanted to get his anger out. His PP was, "Don't you give me any of your back talk."

SOME NOK DISEASE CAUSES

Some major PP's are "Don't feel," "Don't think," "Don't grow up (be my baby),"* "Be afraid," "Be fat like me," "Be stupid," (don't get too smart), "Be stubborn, "Stutter, like me," "Be second," (be a loser), "Be lazy," (you're just like your Uncle Joe, the laziest man on earth). Get the idea what PP's are? They're statements made about or to you, which you believe and which you make work. Other messages from People Less in Charge are "She's no good," (she can't play), "You don't know how," "We don't want him or her on our side," "Clumsy," "Dumb," "Here comes the fumbler," "Strike out king," "You smell," "Fatso," "Big feet," "Freckles," and so on.

*Statements in parentheses ( ) tell the hidden or ulterior message . . .

The onset, as doctors say, of the NOK disease begins with the first NOK message. It gets worse with time because the more you try and are unable to do what people want you to do, the stronger the poison they give you, like "Try harder," (fail)* "You're just plain lazy," (be lazy) "Just like your Uncle Zip," "I'll punish you for being lazy," (be lazy, you're born lazy, doomed to be lazy all your life).

THE PREVENTION AND CURE:

Spotting People Poison is an Adult activity. When you see, hear, or feel one coming at you, you can alert your Child to ward it off. Then C doesn't take the poison and doesn't feel NOK. One way to become an expert NOK spotter is to listen to people talking to their children. Another way is to talk about PP's in class or group.

Most PP messages have a second hidden meaning which you get without knowing it. Here are some PP's I just heard with the hidden message in parentheses ( ).

"My Sioux has a memory like a computer." (be a robot)
"My Jamie is so stubborn," (be stubborn)
"She's really very shy," (be shy)
"You're just a little thief," (be a thief)
"He's a real clown, but he's so cute. (be a clown)

*Statements in parentheses ( ) tell the hidden or ulterior message.

83

Notice these are things parents say about their children, which they usually hear. Have you heard messages like these? Talk about them now. These are the People Poisoning messages which can mess up your whole life. Are you following any like that? Check it out.

TA SHOTS (People Protection)

TA can be like a shot against PP. TA can help you to recognize People Poison instantly. The minute you hear one, it is quite easy to duck it. Of course you must be in your Adult to avoid taking any PP. Then follow up with a P shrinker: give three Warm Fuzzies to the other person's Kid and watch them shift from their Parent into their Child. Ever try stroking your own Parent? Try that. Positive strokes (Warm Fuzzies) are infectious too. It's a nice cure and gets you gold stamps.

MORE PARENT SHRINKERS

Here are other ways to get people who are coming on from their Parent to stop. Try them and see if they work for you. They're called Parent Shrinkers.*

1. Say "You're right. What can we do about it now?" Changes: (P to A)
2. Say "How sharp of you to notice. How can I fix it?" (P to A)
3. Use big words, like: "How perspicacious of you to elucidate so quintessentially." (Doesn't mean anything but it will make them laugh or ask a question.) (P to C or A)
4. Ask "What did you say before you said that?" (P to A)
5. Exaggerate the fault that is being pointed out. (P to C, you hope)
6. Change the subject. (P to A)
7. Leave the room. ("Excuse me. I'll be right back.")
8. Stroke their Kid: "You're cute when you get so angry." (P to C)

*Larry Mart — unpublished manuscript.

You don't have to feel hurt when someone is mean. Be tough. Don't let it hurt. You're OK. If they're mean, that's their problem. Remember when the going gets tough, the tough get going! Are you tough or soft?

In Chapter Ten I suggested a neat way to avoid Games and to get what you want by talking about what you are feeling. When someone does something you don't like, tell them what you would like them to do. This is known in TA language as "coming on straight," and asking for what you want. Some people call it "assertiveness."

Here it is again. If someone calls you a name you can say, "When you (call me a name) I feel (hurt or angry). So I (wish you wouldn't do that). This will get rid of the poison in you immediately and may help to keep them from sending more your way. Try it. No guarantees but it does help sometimes.

EXERCISES

1. Have you heard any PP's? Tell us about them.

2. What is NOK disease?

3. How can you keep from getting NOK disease?

4. How can you get rid of it?

5. What are some Parent Shrinkers?

6. Make up a play with one actor throwing PP's and another using Parent Shrinkers to stop the poison darts.

WORDS AND IDEAS FOR YOUR ADULT

People Poisons

NOK disease

Onset

Protection

Assertiveness

Guarantees

Parent Shrinkers

Exaggerate

Tough

People in Charge

People Less in Charge

A promise made is a debt unpaid.
— Shakespeare

CHAPTER FOURTEEN
Promises, Agreements and Contracts

YOU PROMISED!

Dad said, "When I come home, I'm going to bring you something." When he came home from his trip, after some delay he said, "Oh, yes, I promised to bring you something and I did." What fun that was, and you learned that "promise" meant "You can trust dad to do what he says he'll do."

Then another time he promised to bring you something and didn't. He said, "Oh, I forgot." Now wasn't that awful! On still another occasion he or mother may have said, "I'll bring you something," and you said, "Will you promise?" And they said, "I promise." Then you said, "Do you always keep your promises?" and the person said, "I always keep my promises. I do what I say I'll do." Now you knew that they were going to bring you a gift because they said they *always* keep their promises. Since they always keep their promises, you knew you could depend on them to do what they said they would do.

In the same way, when you make a promise, people know you'll do what you say. Promises are very important. Keeping your promise is even more important if you want people to believe you. Have you ever made a promise? Did you keep it? Why? Why not? Tell about it right now.

CONTRACTS — A TWO-WAY STREET

Have you ever heard grownups say: "I have a new contract with the firm," or "Chris Evert, the famous tennis player, just signed a new contract for a million dollars." So a contract is a legal and official way of putting down on paper what people promise to do for each other. They sign a paper saying they agree to do so much work for a certain amount of money.

TRIERS FAIL, DOERS DO!

Promises are important because if people are not able to trust each other, then everything gets mixed up. People get confused and disappointed and no one knows what to do. To get away from getting mixed up like that, the best idea is for you to say exactly what you intend to do, *and do it*. This builds habits of honesty which people like because they can trust you. Next, let others know what you want. Then, if you both agree, you can make a contract which will keep you from being mixed up. Saying you're going to do something is one thing. Doing it is the important thing. Trying is not the same as doing.

Here's how a contract can work at home: Jim and Sue Blackstone both work; sometimes Jim works late, sometimes Sue does. When Jim gets home first, he starts to cook dinner and when Sue gets home first, she is the cook. That has been their contract for years. But Tammy and Todd argued every day about who was "supposed" to set the table and who "had" to do the dishes. So the four of them sat down and worked out a contract. Todd usually got home late on Monday, Wednesday, and Friday because he played football and softball — so on those days Tammy would set the table and Todd would do the dishes. On Tuesday and Thursday they would exchange jobs. This contract worked out fine and when it didn't, the Blackstone family could sit down together and change it.

EVERYONE HELPS DECIDE

To make a contract work each person must have a part in deciding, feeling it's fair, and agreeing to it. You see, when the Blackstones made the contract about setting the table and doing the dishes, they sat down around the table and agreed about the best way to get the jobs done. They talked about it and each had a part in it. Each felt it was the best and fairest one for them. That way nobody felt that they were cheated and everybody kept the contract. When someone failed to do his part, they talked about that at the next meeting so they could renew the contract.

WE MADE THE CONTRACT

What kinds of contracts do you have at home? About keeping your room neat or coming home from school or taking out the trash? Most mothers and fathers just tell us what to do. They say, "Now here's the way it's going to be." Then we don't feel that we have a part in it and we feel sort of cheated. We feel it's not fair, and that the contract doesn't work because we didn't really promise. We were *told* what to do. So, if the contract is going to work, it's better for the people who agree to it to help build it. Sometimes it doesn't work out for one reason or another. Rather than letting P say, "You broke the contract," you can go back and change the plan. "Well, this didn't work because — so isn't there some other way?" Then you can rework it so that everybody can keep their contract promises.

PROMISES AND TRUST

One last word on promises and trust. Just because you or someone else does not *always* keep a promise *does not* mean that you can never trust them again. Sometimes things happen which keep people from doing what they say they will do. Other times they just forget. Did you ever forget your promise? Yes? Do you always forget your promise? No! Do you remember 90% (9 times out of 10)? 80% of the time? Guess I'd trust you most of the time. Nobody's perfect — nor perfectly awful. Somewhere in between lies the truth. Do you trust you? I do! It's important that you do. Because you won't trust others until you trust yourself.

90

KEEPING OR BREAKING PROMISES

When people grow up they may forget about how important promises are. They break some very serious ones. You have heard of divorces. Well, lots of times divorces occur when people don't keep their promises to each other. Sometimes their sons and daughters feel they caused the divorce and feel awful. That's something to talk about too.

When promises (treaties) between countries are broken, it sometimes leads to war and killing. So agreements and promises are very important and they make contracts work.

In TA groups we try to make our contracts very, very clear. We ask people to tell what they want to accomplish by learning TA. What are you going to work on? What are you going to accomplish, what are you going to change in you? If you can say that, then I can help you to accomplish your goal. The contract between us is clear. Now will you take the time to figure out what kind of contract you have? At home? At school? With your gang?

EXERCISES FOR GROUP

1. A promise is a contract. True or false.

2. An agreement is a contract. True or false.

3. Tell why promises are important to you.

4. Tell why keeping your promise is important to you.

5. What happens when you or someone else fails to keep their promises? Did this ever happen to you? Tell about it. How did you handle it? P, A, or C? What could you have done about it so that everybody came out a winner?

6. Talk about trusting people. Whom do you trust? Did you ever trust someone and they let you down? Could you trust them again? What do you think about when you stop trusting people?

(To find out if you have labeled them correctly turn to page 100 and you'll see the answers.)

WORDS AND IDEAS FOR YOUR ADULT

Promise
Agreement
Contracts
Trust

CHAPTER FIFTEEN
Zoom Free With TA

Being OK is being free to live, to zoom to joy. We've been talking about getting acquainted with yourself, of getting to understand yourself. How neat it would be if you were able to do this, because then you could rap with people and be happier.

You may have learned a great deal about yourself and others while reading this book. You've learned how all of us are made up of three people. These three can talk to each other and to others. Sometimes when we talk, we hurt or get hurt, give or pick up Brown Stamps. Sometimes we play Games and get ourselves and others mixed up. We learned about how there are family Rackets. We learned that to be sad, mad, afraid, or hurt is an OK way to feel and how to express those feelings.

We've learned that people are often unhappy and sad unless they come on straight with each other. If they do that and they care about each other, then they can begin to make more sense, get along better, love each other, and to know that they are OK.

GETTING ALONG WITH OTHERS MEANS FEELING GOOD ABOUT ME!

What we want to talk about now is how to make use of TA so that you can become skilled at helping other people feel OK and, in turn, to feel OK yourself. Here are some of the ways that we use TA. If other people are to feel good, we have to feel good. The first job then is to tell ourselves every day, "I'm OK — You're OK." (Put a bumper sticker on your mirror and read it out loud every morning.) This means that other people are *worthwhile, adequate,* and *important* and so am I. They won't hurt me and I won't hurt them. I can get close to them and love them, and they can get close to me and love me. We can trust each other.

Remind yourself often that all people are OK. Mother and daddy, brothers, sisters, playmates, teachers. Even people who are nasty to us are OK although sometimes they say and do some pretty awful things. That doesn't mean that everything they do pleases me, or everything I do pleases them. It only means that all of us are worthwhile, important, and able to think (OK). If we're able to do that, we don't have to be angry with or afraid of each other.

TRACK DOWN FEELINGS AND AVOID BROWN STAMPS

Wouldn't it feel better if you didn't have to sulk, go around feeling sad, mad, or bad? The reason we do this is because we print and keep Brown Stamps. We talked about Brown Stamps earlier. One way to avoid printing Brown Stamps is to do what is called a "trackdown."* As soon as your Child feels uncomfortable, do a trackdown.

You have seen the arrows that we have drawn to point out what happens to your Child when somebody shoots an arrow at you. They may say or do a mean thing that hurts. So, in order not to take the red arrow which gets shot at you by somebody trying to hurt you and put you down, do a "trackdown."

Here is the way it goes: as soon as you feel uncomfortable, as soon as someone says something that annoys you, as soon as someone does something that frightens you, you can say to yourself "I hurt," and then immediately say "How?" The answer to this question puts you into your Adult. OK? The answer to "How" is "anger," "fear," or "pain."

The next question that you put to yourself is "Which part? P, A, or C?" Usually the answer is "My Child."

Then you can ask, "Who done it?" (Like in a mystery play.) "Who did this to me?" The answer will be the person who sent the arrow like cousin, dad, mother, sister, brother, or somebody.

Then "With what?" (P, A, or C?) Usually, if it is mother or dad, the answer is "Their Parent." OK?

Then, "Why did they do it?" "Because *they* were afraid" or "Because *they* were angry" or "Because *they* were sad and their Child was

*Thanks to Larry Mart, Teaching Member, ITAA, Sacramento, California.

unhappy" or "Because they were acting to protect me or something like that . . ." So, stop to figure out what is going on.

Now the next question is, "What can I do now?" The answer is, "do a trackdown." This keeps you from getting angry, afraid, or sad.

Finally, "What can I do different later?" That's easy. "Avoid hooking other people."

So there we have a trackdown. Learn to do this in thirty seconds. It goes like this:

1. I hurt
2. How?
3. Which part?
4. Who done it?
5. With what?
6. Why did he/she do it?
7. What can I do now?
8. What can I do different later?

By the time you get finished with the thirty second trackdown you won't be angry, you won't be hurt, you won't be afraid, and you won't print any Brown Stamps. You'll feel so much better because you didn't pick up any old, dilapidated, dirty, brown feelings.

KEEPING PEOPLE* BY GIVING STROKES

Another way to use TA is to give a lot of strokes to other people. You know, when we are growing up, we are criticized a great deal. We're told by a lot of people what's wrong with us and so we learn to be criticizers. We are never really taught to tell other people how nice they are or about the good things they do, or what we like about them. In

*From lectures by Larry Mart, Teaching Member, ITAA, Sacramento, California.

fact, we get sort of embarrassed to hear it and we get embarrassed to tell it. If you practice telling other people what you like about them, what you admire, you'll find it easier to do it at home. You'll find that other people begin to like you and like to be with you. There are other ways to "keep people." Find something nice to tell each person you meet. Later think about how it felt to say it and how it felt to be told. How else can you stroke people?

AVOID GAMES

Another way to use TA is to become more aware of the Games that you get involved in. Do you start them or does somebody else? It's important to know how to get out of them. Did you ever get into a Game of "Why don't you, yes but?" with someone else starting it? How annoying when someone asks you to tell them how to do something, and then they tell you what's wrong with it. So, one way of getting out of that Game is not to play. If they ask you what to do, don't give advice and perhaps you won't be sucked into a Game that winds up with you feeling very foolish. When we play Games we waste time and lose friends. If we can keep from playing Games, we can begin to know that other people are OK and that you're OK. Then you will have learned to use TA. You will have learned how to make yourself and the people you love happy.

I hope you have enjoyed reading this book. Keep your Adult plugged in, let your Kid out and have fun. Now get on with living a full wonderful loving life because you know you are OK.

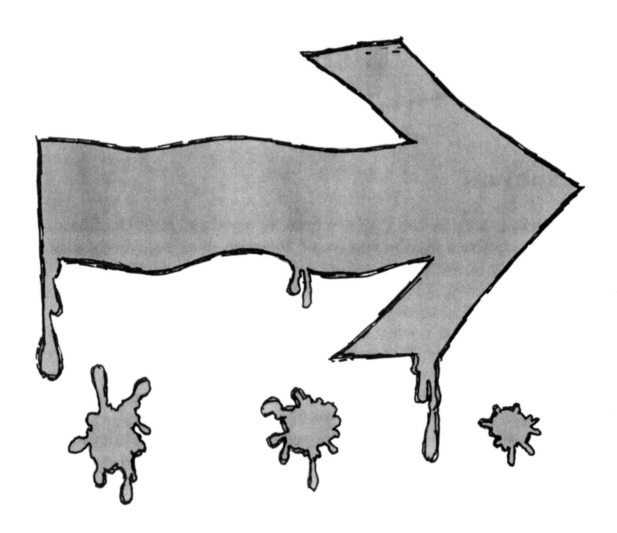

ANSWER SHEET

Chapter One

1. Discussion
2. Parent, Adult, Child
3. Parent means the critical and nurturing part in each of us; parent means mother or father.
4. To understand self and others so as to feel better about one's self and to get along better with others.
5. Discussion

Chapter Three

1. Parent
2. C, C
3. Parent
4. Critical
5. (a) CP   (j) NP
   (b) CP   (k) NP
   (c) CP   (l) NP
   (d) CP   (m) NP
   (e) CP   (n) NP
   (f) CP   (o) NP
   (g) NP   (p) NP
   (h) NP   (g) NP
   (i) NP   (r) NP

Chapter Five

1. Jerk

2. Little Professor
3. Natural or Free
4. Adapted

Chapter Six

1. A
2. A
3. True
4. True
5. True
6. False
7. False

Chapter Nine

1. Stroke
2. Parallel
3. Crossed
4. Fight
5. Double or hidden

Chapter Eleven

1. True
2. False
3. True

Chapter Fourteen

1. True
2. True